GW00692380

Irish
Grave Humour

**Here lies John Higley
whose father and mother were drowned
in their passage from America.
Had they both lived they would have been buried
here.**

Authentic epitaphs that once embellished the graves and tombs
of the deceased in Ireland.
Poignant, funny, heartfelt, they tell us a surprising amount about
those buried underneath. With humour and candidness, they
bring 'to life' the characters from past generations.

**This stone was raised by Sarah's lord
Not Sarah's virtues to record —
For they're well known to all the town
But it was raised to keep her down.**

IRISH GRAVE HUMOUR

An Anthology of Epitaphs

RAYMOND LAMONT-BROWN

THE O'BRIEN PRESS

First published 1987 by
The O'Brien Press
20 Victoria Road, Dublin 6, Ireland.

ISBN 0-86278-153-1

10 9 8 7 6 5 4 3 2 1

Editing and design: Michael O'Brien and Ide O'Leary
Typesetting: Phototype-Set Ltd., Dublin
Printing: Guernsey Press Co. Ltd., Guernsey, Channel Islands.

Contents

Acknowledgements

The author would like to thank the editors and readers of the dozens of Irish publications from the *Catholic Standard* to the *Fermanagh Herald* for their help in collecting many of the epitaphs which appear herein. In particular special thanks go to the broadcaster Gay Byrne and Radio Telefís Eireann for publicising the author's search for the more obscure Irish epitaphs. Thanks, too, go to W. E. Mackey, Research Librarian at Trinity College Library, for help with tracing some of the more academic sources, and to Brian J. Cantwell for bringing the author's attention to epitaphs in Co. Clare, Co. Wexford and Co. Wicklow.

Preface

Lynch's house, Lombard Street, Galway. 'Remember Deathe,
vaniti of vaniti, and all is but vaniti.'

This anthology of Irish epitaphs has been set out to show as many
of man's emotions as possible, so that it forms a book of laughter
and tears, courage and cowardice, confidence and fear, sentiment
and piety, irony and wisdom, wit and humour. The main purpose
of the anthology is to amuse, entertain and interest, for, from the
beginning of time, mankind has been concerned as much with the
past as with the future, spending much time and effort in studying
the history of those who have gone before.

To achieve a balance of subject matter, much editing has been
needed and epitaphs of very similar nature have been sifted and
the best examples chosen. This anthology does not therefore in any
way claim to be an exhaustive work on the subject and it is hoped
that it will be a stimulus to others to explore this underrated
subject.

Levity in the churchyard may seem a strange phenomenon to us
now, but the custom of using churchyards for sport, markets and
pleasure was an old-established and persistent one. There are
records as early as the fourth century of St Basil protesting against
the holding of markets in churchyards on the pretext of making
preparations for festivals. But even though such dignitaries as the

canons of the Synod of Exeter of 1287 strictly asked that parish priests make sure that 'combats, dances or other improper sports ... or stage plays or farces' (*ludos theatrales et ludebriorum spectacula*) were prohibited, the fairs persisted and often ale was brewed on the church premises.

As a secondary theme, and without pretensions to erudition, this book also sets out to explain in simple terms the development of the epitaph in Ireland, what to look for and where to find it.

All the epitaphs which appear in this book are genuine and authentic, in that they all once embellished the graves or tombs of the deceased in Ireland. As time passes, alas, many epitaphs become less and less accessible. Vandalism, weather, rural and urban decay, or church renovation — and several other reasons — may make it that some of the epitaphs herein quoted have been moved from their original sitings. So, the collector should not be surprised or disappointed if they are not found where cited herein. Where no exact site is given, the whereabouts of the epitaph are not known today.

Introducing Irish Epitaphs

How Irish Epitaphs Began

The headstones with their epitaphs that we know today are descendants of the great stone monuments of megalithic Europe, known as menhirs, dolmens and cromlechs. A menhir is a single upright stone which may have been the memorial of an event or a Celtic hero. The dolmen, which means 'table stone', is a stone chamber consisting of several stones set up on edge and covered by a horizontal slab. Such structures may be all that is left of an elongated grave mound called a long-barrow. The cromlech is a ring of standing stones, generally surrounding a menhir or a dolmen.

Ireland's early cemeteries were in sacred places detached from living areas or within the enclosure of *raths* (circular earthworks) or *cashels*. The pagan burial places were gradually abandoned after the introduction of Christianity in the fifth century; the dead were now placed in consecrated cemeteries attached to the primitive churches. The fashions in monuments in pagan cemeteries were carried over to Christian times and several stones still exist with a mixture of pagan decoration and Christian symbolism; one pagan custom which survived for a long time was the placing of a *cairn* of stones over the grave. It was an early wish to be buried on a hill and often the elevation was enhanced by placing a *duma*, or burial-mound, on the hill; here the dead person was placed, perhaps in a shallow stone coffin. Sometimes around the *duma* a circle of pillar-stones was erected. The pillar-stone developed into our headstone with its Christian inscription. The oldest pillar-stone in Ireland, scholars believe — and consequently Ireland's oldest epitaph — is that of Lugnad (Lugna), traditionally identified as the son of the sister of St Patrick, at Templepatrick, Inchagoill, Lough Corrib. It reads:

LIE LUGNAEDON MACC LMENUEH
(The stone of Lugnaed son of Limenueh.)

The earliest of Ireland's epitaphs were in ogham, that curious writing form of twenty-five letters set in combinations of one to five parallel strokes in various positions down a central line. One old Irish epitaph in ogham recorded by the antiquary Dr George Petrie in 1845 reads:

This is Eochaid Airgthech: Caille slew me in an encounter against Finn

Ireland's earliest epitaphs, that most people would recognise as such today, are to be found on the graveslabs of the Early Christian monasteries. These slabs are, generally, flat stones bearing an inscribed cross, or a Chi-Rho monogram, and have an inscription asking for a prayer for the person buried beneath. One such is to be found at Tullylease, Co. Cork, and reads:

QUICUMQUE LEGERIT HUNC
TITULUM ORAT PRO BERECHTUIRE
*(Whoever reads this inscription
let him pray for St Berichter.)*

In his *Chronicles of the Tombs* (1851), Dr T. J. Pettigrew cites what he believed to be the earliest Christian Irish epitaph. He noted the inscription:

C[APIT]I BRECANI

This, set in a cross in a circle, relates to the sixth-century St Brecon.

Newgrange, Co. Meath, with its own special kind of epitaph.

The Druid's Altar dolmen, Island Magee,
Co. Antrim.

Ogham stone, Ballintaggart, Co. Kerry.

The earliest royal epitaphs in Ireland may be found at such sites as the monastery of Clonmacnois; for example Dr George Petrie collected one in his *Christian Inscriptions* (1872):

OROIT DI CONAING
MAC CONGHAIL
(Pray for Conaing, son of Conghal.)

Conghal was king of Tessia. In the case of non-royal folk, the family name and profession is rarely mentioned in Early Irish Christian epitaphs.

One of the earliest of the Early Christian cemeteries in Ireland is marked out by the Kilnasaggart Pillar Stone, Co. Armagh, on the ancient roadway of *Slighe Miodhluachra*. It has an Irish inscription dedicating the place to Ternoch, son of Ceran Bic. Still to be seen are several small cross-carved slabs which were probably grave-markers before the use of lettered epitaphs.

County Tyrone has one of the most exclusive cemeteries anywhere — Relignaman graveyard, Carrickmore, was reserved entirely for women. It is said to have originated from the tradition that St Columba insisted that all 'wicked' women should be buried out of earshot of his bell!

Epitaphs developed through the fashions relating to tombstones. It should be remembered too, that although Pope Gregory the Great authorised relatives to erect tablets with epitaphs on graves (for prayers for the welfare of the souls of the dead), graveyards for the ordinary man and woman did not appear until the seventh century and commemorative stones much later. At that time burials inside churches were mainly reserved for ecclesiastics and religious dignitaries.

The recumbent effigy figure on tombs was brought to Ireland by the Anglo-Normans and was very popular until the thirteenth century. These tombs, with their simple Latin epitaphs, tell us a lot about the fashions and customs of the times. By the fourteenth century however, the rich carved stone canopy tomb had made its debut.

Epitaphs of medieval times mirrored the Early Christian ones in that they were usually in the form of tender prayers both for the living and the dead, whereas those of the Elizabethan and

Norman knight on tombstone at Old Kilcullen Church, Co. Kildare.

Jacobean eras were more often historical and stated who a person was and what he or she did. From 1600 to *circa* 1650 epitaphs were poetic, changing to inscriptions of one line or phrase under Cromwell. During the period 1660 to 1680 epitaphs become long-winded. As a rule the most humorous of the epitaphs extant today date from 1700 to around 1760.

Ireland has a wide range of examples for the tomb hunter and these are worth mentioning in their historical periods. There is an eleventh-century monument worthy of note at Bangher Old Church, Magheramore, Co. Derry. It is a steep pitch tomb of St Muiredach O'Heney, founder of the church. Another early one is the twelfth-century effigy of Thomas de Cantwell at Kilfare, Co. Kilkenny. The thirteenth and fourteenth centuries produced flat or hog-backed slabs with floriated crosses and marginal inscriptions, which are contemporary with the English cross-slabs. Sometimes the inscriptions of this period were on the stems of stone crosses in Norman-French, Latin or English, but never Irish. The lettering was Lombardic or Gothic. Altar tombs were popular in this period, some of great elaboration, but few are of

The tomb of the O'Cahan chieftain, Dungiven, Co. Derry.

artistic or technical merit. These were for aristocratic folk, as the common people, up to the fifteenth century, did not commemorate their dead.

The tomb at the priory church of Dungiven, Co. Derry, of an O'Cahan chieftain who died in 1385, is worthy of mention here. His is a recess tomb, with effigy and traceried canopy; six standing figures represent his sons. From the fifteenth century the tomb of the MacMahons of *circa* 1475 (reconstructed 1843) might be noted too at Ennis Franciscan Friary, Co. Clare, and the one to the Lawrence family, *circa* 1477, at St Mary's Church, Howth, Co. Dublin.

From the mid-fifteenth century to the mid-seventeenth century the incised slab in Latin or English started to appear for the poorer folk; these were the craft slabs for smiths, ploughmen and so on. From the later date the tombstone of John Tobyn at St Mary's Church, Callan, Co. Kilkenny, ought to be cited and the tomb of Sir Arthur Chichester at the church of St Nicholas, Carrickfergus, Co. Antrim. The sixteenth century saw the rise of sculptors who designed particular tombstones. One such was Rory O'Tunney whose *circa* 1526 tomb to Piers Fitz Oge Butler at the Cistercian Abbey at Kilcooley, Co. Tipperary, is a fine example. At St Mochuda's Cathedral, Lismore, Co. Waterford, there is a fine individualised tomb to the MacGrath family showing a rare example of named figures.

The seventeenth century in Ireland saw the flat slabs giving way to more ornate tombstones and the embellishment of stones with the symbols of death. Symbols have a rich history in Irish churchyards and their environs. The most popular symbols were the spade and the scythe, the all-seeing-eye within a serpent, an open book with quill pen, the skull and crossbones, the death's head above an hour glass and the winged angel of death.

Looking for Epitaphs

It is not a platitude to say that the richest source of epitaphs is the burial ground, for epitaphs seem to crop up in the most unlikely places. In the main the oldest graves in churchyards are to be found at the south side of the church, as people wished to avoid the shadow of the church falling on their graves. This was considered very unlucky, and the north was also associated with the devil — that is the main reason why suicides were buried to the north of a churchyard to act as a first line of defence against the devil. Superstition therefore may be cited as the explanation why churchyards are often higher on the south side than the north, or higher than the road outside the church door-sill; for it was the medieval custom to bury the dead on top of others, and so gradually the ground became elevated. At Carrickmore there were separate cemeteries for suicides, children and slain soldiers.

Besides the town and church graveyards other likely places to look for epitaphs include castle cemeteries and fort burial grounds; two examples worth a look are at Fethard Castle, Co. Tipperary, and Duncannon Fort, Co. Wexford. The latter shows how gravestones were often used for purposes other than marking the resting places of the dead, such as for paths and lintels, fireplaces and wall repairs. One graveyard worthy of a visit for the wide chronology of epitaphs is at Glendalough, Co. Wicklow; it exhibits epitaphs from royal tombs (at Reefert, possibly eleventh century) to nineteenth-century examples.

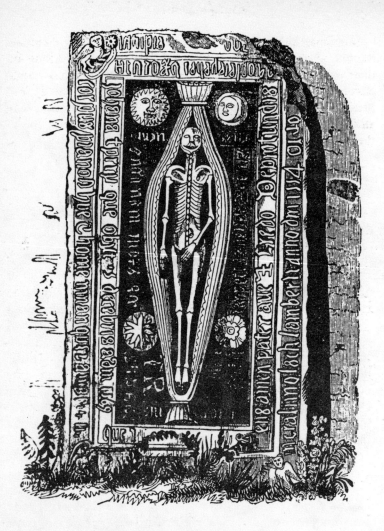

A 'modest' skeleton, Christ Church, Cork.

What Epitaphs Tell Us

Fundamentally, the objective of headstones is to give details of the persons buried below. Most people have some curiosity about their family roots and set about finding out more about them. Several books have been published on how to discover family history, but few give proper emphasis to the most vital and underrated first step, the tracking down of family tombs. This is the range of information an epitaph can give:

<table>
<tr><td></td><td>HERE LYETH ENTOMBED</td></tr>
<tr><td>Name</td><td>JOHN O'DOWD</td></tr>
<tr><td>Occupation</td><td>SCHOOLMASTER</td></tr>
<tr><td>Birthplace</td><td>AND NATIVE OF BALLYNACOLE</td></tr>
<tr><td></td><td>WHO DEPARTED THIS LIFE</td></tr>
<tr><td>Date of death</td><td>THE 7 OF DECEMBER 1703</td></tr>
<tr><td>Age</td><td>AND OF HIS AGE: 63</td></tr>
<tr><td>Marriage</td><td>HIS WIFE MARY O'ROURKE</td></tr>
<tr><td></td><td>PLACED THIS STONE.</td></tr>
<tr><td>Deceased's interests</td><td>Ah John what changed since I saw thee last,</td></tr>
<tr><td></td><td>Thy fishing and thy shooting day are past.</td></tr>
<tr><td></td><td>Thy pen and pencil thou cans't weild no more,</td></tr>
<tr><td>Deceased's character</td><td>Thy nods, grimaces, winks and pranks are o'er.</td></tr>
<tr><td>Wife's dates</td><td>AND TO MARY O'ROURKE</td></tr>
<tr><td></td><td>WIFE OF THE ABOVE</td></tr>
<tr><td></td><td>BORN: 1665   DIED: 1712</td></tr>
<tr><td>Decendant</td><td>AND ONLY DAUGHTER</td></tr>
<tr><td></td><td>MARY</td></tr>
<tr><td></td><td>BORN: 1690   DIED: 1766</td></tr>
</table>

And there's more to epitaphs than that. For throughout the centuries Irish epitaphs have provided a fascinating insight into the rural and social history of their time. Today epitaphs in Irish town and country churchyards show as well as any verse the many emotions of man, so that any handful of epitaphs is a collation of tears and laughter, wisdom grave and wit light, fear and courage.

Epitaphs fit every mood. Quite often epitaphs are all that is left of a local ballad or folk rhyme; no less are they important for telling us something about local people — who they were, what they did and what standing they had amongst their relatives and friends.

Here is an example of an epitaph which is the only remaining sample of the work of a local poet. It was written by an Irish landowner called Henry Tighe in memory of a wood-ranger on his estate at Rosanna, Co. Wicklow:

To the Memory of William Ralph of Kilkenny, who died 21st February 1818, aged 71 years

Guard of the wood in settled low content,
Lived William Ralph, a ramble paid his rent.
A boy, in sportive toil he climbed the trees;
A man, he lov'd them rustling in the breeze.

As he grew old, his old companions spread
A broader, browner shadow o'er his head;
While those he planted shot on high, and made
For many a rook an hospitable shade.

With this one change, life gently crept away,
A placid stream it flowed from day to day.
His friends and children lov'd him, as the tear
Well spoken, profusely shed upon his bier.

If he had faults, thou also have thy share;
Strike thine own breast, and feel what lurketh there.
He who sees all, shall judge both him and thee;
Repent, for as it falls, so lies the tree.

Epitaphs too, can tell us about Ireland's disasters. Here is an example from St Dubhan's church tower, Hook, Co. Wexford: 'Erected to the Memory of Wm Cobhead, Master of the barke *Esther* of Liverpool, who with some of his crew were lost on this Coast in the fearful gale on Sunday, the 20th April 1822'.

As well as giving birth-death details of the deceased, epitaphs have been used for other purposes. In his *English Bards and Scotch Reviews*, Lord Byron (1788-1824) counselled never to believe 'an epitaph, Or any other thing that's false', and Alexander Pope (1688-1744) cursed those who 'taught epitaphs to lie'. For centuries epitaphs have been used as tools of propaganda and none was more blatant than that in the graveyard of the Covenanting Meeting House at Bailie's Mill, Drumbeg, Co. Down, on the tomb of William Graham of Creevy who died in 1828, aged 63. He wrote these lines for his tomb himself to justify his position:

First. I leave my testimony against all the errors of Popery which constitute the Man of Sin and Son of Perdition. Whom my Lord shall destroy by the brightness of His coming.

Secondly. Against Prelacy now set on the throne of Britain, which shall shortly fall like Dagon by the sword of Him who sits on the white horse. For this end, Oh thou Mighty God, gird thy sword upon thy thigh, and thy right-hand shall teach Thee terrible things.

Thirdly. I testify against all who deal falsely in the cause of Christ; all who own the Covenant National and Solemn League, and yet sware allegiance to the support of Prelacy. Oh Lord, take to Thee and rule the Nations, and destroy these two great Idols, Popery and Prelacy, with that rod of Iron Thou hast received from Thy Father.

Lastly. I testify against all opposers of the Covenanted cause, all who have departed from Reformation, and I die giving my full approbation of that cause, for which the Martyrs suffered, and which they sealed with their blood.
Arise, Oh Lord, and plead thy own cause.

Graham was a fanatical supporter of the Covenanting cause —
those pledged to uphold the Presbyterian faith against prelacy and
popery — and cites the smiting of Dagon; Dagon was one of the
gods of the Phoenician creation legend.

How to Date an Epitaph

Dating epitaphs is generally very easy, since most of them have
dates carved on them. If a headstone has no date — if perhaps the
figuring has been weathered — it must be compared with other
dated examples from the point of view of style. Quite often the
lettering gives a good clue; for instance the more cursive
eighteenth-century lettering gave way to small capitals in Regency
times and thence to the bold capitals of the Victorian interments.

Some types of headstone are made of substances other than
stone, like iron, wood or slate; iron and wooden headstones are
very rare. If the latter are undated they tend to be of eighteenth-
century origin. Before headstones came into vogue small
footstones were used, carved with initials; but these can be difficult
to date as they were used by the poor right up to modern times.

Epitaph dates themselves are useful in plotting events in local
history before parish or governmental records began. For instance,
as the compulsory registration of deaths was not established in
Ireland until 1863, epitaph dates help plot mortality. An
assessment might show that during the years 1831-41 in Ireland,
merchants and prosperous folk could hope to enjoy a life
expectancy of 55-60 years, whereas the poor expired at 35-40
years.

Understanding Epitaphs

Decoding some old epitaphs can be difficult as some of them are in Latin. As a guide here are a few of the most common phrases used:

A.D. — Anno Domini: In the Year of Our Lord . . .
Ad maiorem Dei gloriam: For the greater glory of God (the motto of the Society of Jesus).
Adsum: Here I am.
Aetatis suae: Of his (or her) age. On its own *aetatis* means 'of the age', while *aetatis suae* means 'in the particular year of a person's life'. Many tombstones had such inscriptions as 'DIED AETATIS SUAE 87', or 'AS 87'. Sometimes the expression appeared as *anno aetatis suae* (in the year of his or her age).
Aeternum vale: Farewell forever.
Amicus humani generis: A humanitarian, a philanthropist.

Beatae memoriae: Of blessed memory.

Consummatum est: It is completed. (Christ's last words on the cross, John 19:30).

Dei gratia: By the grace of God.
De mortuis nihil nisi bonum: Speak kindly of the dead.
Deo favente: With God's favour. Sometimes appears on gravestones as an alternative to *Deo gratias* (Thanks to God).
Deus misereatur: May God have mercy.
Domino optimo maximo: To the Lord God, supreme ruler of the world (the motto of the Benedictine Order).
Durante vita: During life.

Errare humanum est: To err is human.
Et sequentes (sequentia); And those that follow.
Ex voto: According to one's wishes.

Fama semper vivat: May his (or her) good name live forever.
Fecit: Made it.
Floruit (often expressed as fl.): He (or she) flourished. This is sometimes placed on tombstones when the exact date of birth is unknown.

Besides the town and church graveyards other likely places to look for epitaphs include castle cemeteries and fort burial grounds; two examples worth a look are at Fethard Castle, Co. Tipperary, and Duncannon Fort, Co. Wexford. The latter shows how

Hic jacet: Here lies.
Hoc loco: In this place.

In memoriam: In memory of ...
In perpetuum: Forever. Sometimes *in perpetuo*.

Natus est: Born.

Obiit: He or she died.
Obiit sine prole: He or she died without issue.

Requiescat in pace: May he or she rest in peace. Sometimes as *Requiescant in pace* (May they rest in peace).

Respice finem: Look before you leap. The full adage from which this is taken is *Quidquid agas prudenter agas et respice finem* (Whatever you do, do with caution, and look to the end).

Resurgam: I shall rise again.

Sic transit gloria mundi: So passes away the glory of the world. A popular epitaph taken from *De Imitatione Christi* by Thomas à Kempis, the German mystic.

Siste viator: Stop, traveller.

Sit tibi terra levis: May the earth be light upon you.

Terra es, terram ibis: Dust thou art, to dust thou shalt return. Some Irish Victorians incorporated a stanza from the poem *A Psalm of Life* by the American poet Henry Wadsworth Longfellow in their tombstone inscription.

> Life is real! Life is earnest!
> And the grave is not its goal;
> Dust thou art, to dust returnest,
> Was not spoken of the soul.

Tempus fugit: Time flies.

Vixit . . . annos: He or she lived (a certain number of) years.

Relationships

Pater: Father
Socer: Father-in-law
Mater: Mother
Socrus: Mother-in-law
Filius: Son
Gener: Son-in-law
Filia: Daughter
Nursus: Daughter-in-law
Uxor: Wife
Maritus: Husband
Patrius: Uncle
Amita: Aunt
Consobrinus: Cousin (*m*)

Consobrina: Cousin (*f*)
Homo: Man
Femina: Woman
Infans: Child
  puer — Boy
  puella — Girl
Avus: Grandfather
Avia: Grandmother

(There are alternative Latin words to express the same relation, but these are the most common on epitaphs.)

24

Roman Numerals

1: I	20: XX
2: II	30: XXX
3: III	40: XL
4: IV	50: L
5: V	60: LX
6: VI	70: LXX
7: VII	80: LXXX
8: VIII	90: XC
9: IX	100: C
10: X	200: CC
11: XI	300: CCC
12: XII	400: CD
13: XIII	500: D
14: XIV	600: DC
15: XV	700: DCC
16: XVI	800: DCCC
17: XVII	900: CM
18: XVIII	1000: M
19: XIX	1500: MD
	1800: MDCCC
	1900: MCM

(Thus 1674 would be expressed MDCLXXIV, or 1962 as MCMLXII.)

A little knowledge of Latin can unlock some interesting stories set in epitaphs. Take for instance the epitaph of Miler Magrath, Roman Catholic Bishop of Down, who turned coat to become Protestant Archbishop of Cashel. This erstwhile Franciscan wrote himself an epitaph which was set on his tomb at Cashel Cathedral. He died in 1621 aged 100, and wrote a mystery into the last couplet of his epitaph:

VENERAT IN DUNUM PRIMO SANCTISSIMUS OLIM
PATRICIUS NOSTRI GLORIA MAGNA SOLI
HUIC EGO SUCCEDENS, UTINAM TAM SANCTUS UT
ILLE
SEC DUNI PRIMO TEMPORE PRAESUL ERAM.
ANGLIA LUSTRA DECEM SED POST TUA SCEPTA
COLEBAM,
PRINCIPIBUS PLACUI MARTE TONANTE TUIS
HIS UBI SUM POSITUS NON SUM, SUM NON UBI NON
SUM.
SUM NEC IN AMBOBUS SUM NEC UTROQUE LOCI.

Which may be rendered:

Patrick, the glory of our isle and gown,
First sat a bishop in the see of Down.
I wish that I, succeeded him in place
As bishop, had an equal share of grace,
I served thee, England, fifty years in jars
And pleased thy princes in the midst of wars.
Here where I'm placed I'm not; and thus the case is
I'm not in both, yet am in both the places.

Some historians think that the last two lines suggest that the Archbishop had a reversal of faith at the end and had his body buried elsewhere.

Epitaphs on Monumental Brasses

Epitaphs and church memorials engraved on brass were utilised during the Middle Ages as an alternative to the usual tombstones and plaques. The heyday of such monumental brasses was the period from the thirteenth to the eighteenth century. For the purist the material used was not brass as we know it but latten (or bronze) made up of an amalgam of copper, zinc, lead and tin. Much of the work was imported from the Low Countries and Germany. Usually the brasses were of four categories: knights; ladies and husbands; civilians, merchants, scholars; and miscellaneous, which took in symbols of death from skeletons to shrouds.

Today Ireland sports only five medieval brasses, four in St Patrick's Cathedral and one in Christchurch Cathedral, Dublin. The one at Christchurch Cathedral is a rectangular plate with small achievement (heraldic device) and is dated *circa* 1580; it shows the sons of Sir Arthur Grey — two children and one chrysom (a baby in swaddling clothes). The four in St Patrick's are:

1528. Dean Robert Sutton, kneeling and wearing an almuce (a fur cape with a collar and long tails in front); this is a quadrangular plate showing the Trinity.

1537. Dean Geoffry Fyche, kneeling and dressed like his predecessor Dean Sutton; the symbolism herein is of the Blessed Virgin as Our Lady of Pity.

1579. Sir Edward Fiton and his wife Anne and their nine sons. Civilian dress appears on this brass.

1580. Lady and infant.

The inscriptions connected with the early brasses were in Norman-French and were set out in Lombardic letters around the stonework of the slab mounting. From the 1350s, the inscriptions were set out on brass strips, the language used being Latin, with much abbreviation. A common phrase on the mountings was: *Cujus animae propicietur deus, amen,* which was abbreviated to *Cui.aie.ppict'.ds.Am.* When the inscriptions are placed on the marginal fillet, the corners are usually embossed with the four evangelist figures — St Mark (the winged lion), St Matthew (the angel), St Luke (the winged bull), St John (the eagle), each figure holding a scroll. Several of Ireland's other churches have brasses but these are usually of Victorian date and are simple 'name and age' descriptions.

Brass monument of Dean Sutton, St Patrick's Cathedral.

Where to Begin

No serious study of Irish epitaphs *in situ* would be complete without examining the fascinating material collected by the Association for the Preservation of the Memorials of the Dead in Ireland. This Association was the brainchild of Col. Philip Doyne Vigors (1825-1903) and was a piece of inspiration that all local historians should be grateful for. Vigors and his correspondents preserved on record many hundreds of epitaphs which have now either vanished or are in a bad state of repair. The Association's journal is a mine of information on tombs and epitaphs. The details of the publication are: *Irish Memorials of the Dead*, Ed. P. D. Vigors & c, Vols I (1888)-XIII(1) 1934. These offer a good starting point for any subsequent field study.

A Polite Reminder

*Remember, when you exploring for epitaphs, a churchyard is after all a **church**-yard. Treat it with reverence and you will be welcomed by the church officers.*

Ireland's Most Popular
Epitaph

In the graveyard of Roslea, Co. Fermanagh, is this epitaph:

> Dear Friend as you pass by
> As you are now so once was I.
> As I am now so you must be
> Prepare the way to follow me.

The sentiment of this epitaph is very old and is mirrored all over Ireland, making it, because of the number of occurrences, undoubtedly Ireland's favourite. It is based on the famous advice from the Roman satirist and poet Quintus Horatius Flaccus, who lived 65 B.C. to 8 B.C. and is known to us as Horace; in his *Odes* he said, *Carpe diem, quam minimum credula postero* (Enjoy today, trusting little in tomorrow).

Old Irish epitaphs reflected the above advice in two main ways:

> Hodie mihi, cras tibi
> (My turn today, yours tomorrow)

and . . .

> Memento, homo, quia pulvis es et in pulverem revertis.
> (Remember, man, that dust thou art, and to dust shalt thou
> return)

the latter being the Latin way of saying the words in *Genesis* which

God spoke to Adam.

At Mullary, above five miles north of Drogheda, Co. Louth, is this version:

> **Remember Man as you pass by,**
> **As you are now so once was I,**
> **As I am now so you will be,**
> **Prepare for Death and Follow me.**

A wag added these words (now removed):

> To Follow you I am content
> But I'm damned if I know
> Which way you went.

On the back of a tombstone in the churchyard in Ballintubbert, Athy, Co. Kildare, is this variation:

> Stop stranger stop as you pass by,
> As you are now so once was I,
> As I am now so shall you be,
> Prepare yourself for Eternity.

> For life at best is but a crooked street,
> Death the market place where all must meet,
> If life were merchandise that gold would buy
> The rich would live
> The poor alone would die.

At Old Kilcullen, Co. Kildare, the epitaph writer has mirrored the basic theme but left a last line that does not scan:

> Ye wiley youths, as you pass by,
> Look on my grave with weeping eye:
> Waste not your strength before it blossom
> For if you do yous will shurdley want it.
> *(Collected by J. F. Ferguson, Dublin, 1853)*

At Aughnacliffe Churchyard, Co. Longford, and dated 1822, there is a more personalised version:

> Here lies the body of John Carey.
> Remember man as you pass by
> As I am now, so will you be.
> So think on death and pray for me.

Carey was a local school teacher and something of a poet; thus, it is likely that he reworked the lines himself.

Another sentiment was expressed in an epitaph at Templesque 'Church of the Water' Graveyard, Glanmire, Co. Cork, but there the old folk tied it in with an old superstition. The old saw stated that the last person buried in Templesque 'had to draw the water' for all the people in the churchyard until the next person was buried therein. When two funerals took place within a short time of each other the old folk used to say 'He (or she) was not long drawing the water'.

So well known must the doggerel have been that it remained in the mind of one Irish family when they went abroad. On a headstone at Kurrajong Churchyard, near Sydney, Australia, this is to be found:

> Charles Larry is my name,
> Ireland is my nation.
> Wexford is my native place,
> And Christ is my salvation.
>
> Good people all
> As you pass by
> As you are now
> So once was I.
> As I am now
> You soon will be
> Prepare thyself
> To follow me.

From Clondegad:

> Here lies the body of John Glasclune
> While loved and liked by all who knew him.
> In his youth a chatty lad,
> Lies sleeping here in Clondegad.
> All you young men as you pass by,
> As you are now so once was I
> And as I am now so you will be,
> Remember this and pray for me.

Just Restin'

Written by himself

> — *Ballyporeen Churchyard, Tipperary*

On Teague O'Brien
Here I at length repose,
My spirit now at aise is,
With the tips of my toes
And the point of my nose
Turn'd up to the roots of the daises.

The Dairyman's Daughter

> — *Mount Jerome Cemetery, Dublin*

This lonely bud, so young and fair,
Call'd hence by early doom,
Just came to show how sweet a flower
In Paradise might bloom.

On Miss Rose

> — *Bantry, Co. Cork*

Here lies a Rose, a budding Rose,
Blasted before its Bloom,
Whose innocence did sweets disclose,
Beyond that flower's perfume.

To those who for her loss are grieved,
This consolation's given,
She's from a world of woe relieved,
And blooms as Rose in Heaven.

Sacred to the memory of Mrs Maria Boyle

— Bandon, Co. Cork

Who was a good wife, a devoted mother,
And a kind and charitable neighbour.
She painted in water colours,
And was the first cousin to the Earl of Cork,
And such is the Kingdom of Heaven.

Safe under the stone

— Kilmurry Co. Clare
(Collected by Ronald MacDonald Douglas, 1936)

**This stone was raised by Sarah's lord,
Not Sarah's virtues to record —
For they're well known to all the town,
But it was raised to keep her down.**

Paddy saves his breath

— Mayne Cemetery, Clougherhead, Co. Louth

Beneath this stone here lieth one,
That still his friends did please,
To heaven, I hope, he is surely gone,
To enjoy eternal ease.

He drank, he sang while here on earth,
Lived happy as a lord.
And now he hath resigned his breath,
God rest him, Paddy Ward.

(It is maintained in the locality that when this epitaph was inscribed on the stone, some time in the late 1770s, the then parish priest objected to it. The priest order the local stone mason to erase it. This was done and the family of Paddy Ward were enraged and had it reinscribed. Today the addition can still be seen in the depression on the stone which formed the deletion.)

During the 1880s the Rev. Thomas Pegg made a visit to Ireland and his itinerary included Dublin, Maynooth, Mullingar, Ballymahon, Athlone, Birr, Monasterevin and Naas. During that trip he visited as many parish churches as he could and walked around their graveyards. The Rev. Pegg was a keen epitaph hunter and he jotted down his findings in a leatherbound notebook. His gleanings were hilarious and showed a wide range of fine examples of graveyard wit. In that irritating way that Victorians had, though, he was not specific as to the exact locations of the epitaphs he found, so, all that can be said today is that they represent the grave humour of eastern Ireland.

Here are some examples of what the Rev. Pegg discovered:

Here lies, praise God, a woman who
Scolded and stormed her whole life through:
Tread gently o'er her rotting form
Or else you'll raise another storm.

★　★　★

Death will'd that *Thomas Willing* here should lie
Although unwilling he to die.

★　★　★

Here lies one Thomas Foote
Whose bones may hundreds save
For death now has one foot
Entombed within the grave.

★　★　★

Here lies a woman
No man can deny it.

★　★　★

Dear friends and companions all
Pray warning take from me.
Don't venture on the ice too far
For 'twas the death of me.

★　★　★

Weep not for me, my husband dear
Keep it in mind that I lies here.
And when thou'st scour'd and cleaned and pined
Think on why I left it all behind.

★　★　★

**Youth was his age
Virginity his state
Learning his love
Consumption his fate.**

★　★　★

He angles still

— Youghal, Co. Cork

Here lies poor but honest Cecil Pratt.
He was a most expert angler, until death, envious of his merit,
Threw out his line, hooked him, and landed him here.

(This is an unusual example of a modern epitaph which says more
than just name and dates. It is dated 14 June 1973, and gives Cecil
Pratt's age as 67.)

Ancient advice

*— Ardglass, Co. Down, on one of the family of
Lewis Janes, Bishop of Killaloe*

LIVE TO DIE
AND FER THE LORD
AMEND YO LIFE
AND SINE NO MORE
FOR DETHE IS
YE REWARDE
BE PASIENT
IN WEIL A WO
WHEN IS THE END

† † †

BUT FAST A PRE
A WACHE TH… *(defaced)*
MARI JANE MOTHER TO
THOMAS JANES GENTLEMAN
AD 1585

A wise precaution

— The Catholic priest turned Protestant and turned
Catholic again, one Rev. John Pastull, prepared this
epitaph for himself while still alive; it is in St Michael's
Churchyard, Graiguenamanagh, Co. Kilkenny.

Great king of Glory
Justice, Mercy, Peace.
I vilest sinner of the human race
Thou hast prevented
My request thou hast given
It's of Thy Mercy Infinite
That I am among the livin'.
Glory be to the Father and to the Son
And to the Holy Ghost.
JOHN PASTULL AGED 78 YEARS, 1766.

A grave warning

— Duncannon Fort, Co. Wexford

UNDER LYETH THE BODY OF ELIZABETH
TIMPSON, WIFE OF CAPTN TIMPSON
WHO DIED YE 24TH MAY 1736
AGED 31 YEARS
God bless ye hands that lay'd this stone,
And curs'd be the hands that moves her bones.

A razor slipped

— Ennis, Co. Clare

Here lies, alas, poor Roger Norton,
Whose sudden death was oddly brought on.
Trying one day his corns to mow off,
The razor slipped and cut his toe off.
The toe, or rather what it grew to,
The part then took to mortifying
Which was the cause of Roger's dying.

Lines on a stubborn husband

— Dundalk, Co. Louth

Here lies the body of Robert Moore
What signifies more words?
He killed himself by eating curds
But if he'd been ruled by Sarah, his wife,
He might have lived out all the days of his life.

From a double bed to a double grave

— Castlebar, Co. Mayo

To these, whom death again did wed
This grave's the second marriage bed;
For though the hand of fate could force
'Twixt soul and body a divorce,
It would not sever man and wife
Because they both lived but one life.
Peace, good reader, do not weep;
Peace, the lovers are asleep;
They, sweet turtles! folded lie
In the last knot that love could tie;
Let them sleep, let them sleep on
Till this stormy night be gone
And the eternal morrow dawn;
Then the curtains will be drawn
And they wake into a light
Whose day shall never die in night.

Water on the brain

— Abbeyleix, Co. Laois

The illness laid not in one spot,
But through his frame it spread.
The fatal disease was in his heart,
And water in his head.

On a bachelor

— Portlaoise, Co. Laois

At threescore winters' end I died
A cheerless being, sole and sad,
The nuptial knot I never tied —
And wished my father never had.

Kicked into eternity

— Killarney, Co. Kerry

**To all my friends I bid adieu
A more sudden death you never knew
As I was leading the old mare to drink
She kicked and killed me in a wink.**

A traffic accident

— *Cahir, Co. Tipperary*

**Oh Lord, here I lie, and no wonder I'm dead
A thumping great waggon went over my head.**

Peace at last

— *Rath Luirc, Co. Cork*

Underneath this tuft doth lie
Back to back my wife and I.
Generous stranger, spare the tear
For could she speak, I cannot hear.
Happier far than when in life
Free from noise and free from strife
When the last trump the air doth fill
If she gets up then I'll lie still.

The thankful husband

— *Cookstown, Co. Tyrone*

**Death appeared in lovely form,
To bring the calm and end the storm.**

(The husband who wrote this also erected a second stone in
England with similar epitaph for his second wife.)

The cosmopolitan

— *Knockcroghery, Co. Roscommon*

'Been everywhere else'.

Tears at this stone

— Kilkeel Churchyard, Co. Down

Thou wert a sweet winning child,
And wise beyond thy years —
Thy Father's pride, thy Mother's joy,
For thee fast fall our tears.

An intellectual and his wife

— Grangebeg, Templeboy, Co. Sligo

Here lie Tom and his wife Mary,
His surname Burne, hers was Farry.
She modest was, to strangers good
He Greek and Latin understood.
As they shar'd freely what was giv'n
Pray that their souls may rest in Heav'n.

Four gifts

— John Genet of Oldbridge, Co. Meath

The Poore have his Almes
The Worlde has his Praise
The Heavens have his Soule, and
The grave has his Bodie . . . 1690.

On Catherine Gunning

— Castlepollard Church, Rathgraffe, Co. Meath

Here underlies too sad a truth
Discretion innocence and youth
Death veil thy face thy cruel dart
Has virtue pierced thro' beauty's heart.

And, on neighbouring stones:

Twelve years was I a maid,
One year was I a wife;
Half an hour I was a mother,
And then I lost my life.

★   ★   ★

Here lies a famous belly-slave,
Whose mouth was wider than his grave:
Reader, tread lightly o'er his sod,
For, should he gape, you're gone, By God.

Searching for a rhyme

— St Paul's, Bray, Co. Wicklow

The grass is green the rose is red
Here lies my name now I am dead.
Mary Saunders.

In memory of a paragon

— *Modreeny, Co. Tipperary*

In memory of
Louisa, wife of Fredk Falkiner
who died 27th of April 1817
Aged 56
The rectitude of Her Disposition
was equalled by
the mildness of her Temper
And the kindness of Her Affections,
and all were so excellent that in 22 Years
Her Partner never saw Her in ill humour
never heard Her express an unkind word
or do an act
that Reason might not approve
Blessed with such a Companion
possessed of so true a Friend
what should Her Husband fear
but Her Loss?
what should He Dread
but to survive Her?

A Puzzle to All

In the 1860s the publisher Samuel Palmer toured southern Ireland and noted this strange epitaph:

Bene
AT. HT: HIS S. T.
Oneli ESKA
THARI Neg Rayc
Hang'd
F.R.
O! mab V. Syli Fetol
If. Ele
SS. CL.
Ayb. ye AR
Th aN
Dcl — Ays
Hego
Therp. Elfa
ND
NO WS. HE'stur
N'D Toe ART
HH. ERsel Fy
EWEE ... Pin
Gfr ... I ... En
D.S.L.
Et mea D

VI
Seab ATE yo
VRG
RIE Fan
DD
Ryy O! V ... Rey
Esf. OR. WH
ATA
wAi ... TSaflo
O! Doft Ears W.
Ho kNO wS
b uT
ina RVNO
Fy Ears
In. So ... Metall-
Pit ... C
Hero ... R ... broa
D. P.
ans. He ... I
N.H.
Ers Hopma
Y.B.
E. AG ... AIN.

For a long time he and his friends puzzled over the inscription. Was it some kind of Latin code? AT.HT.HIS.S.T and Esf.OR, WH — what did it mean? And then the penny dropped.

This is what the cryptic letters said:

> Beneath this stone lies Katharine Gray,
> Chang'd from a busy life to lifeless clay.
> By earth and clay she got her pelf.
> And now she's turn'd to earth herself.
>
> Ye weeping friends — let me advise —
> Abate your grief, and dry your eyes.
> For what awaits a flood of tears?
> Who knows, but, in a run of years,
> In some tall pitcher or broad pan,
> She in her shop may be again.

Of Merchants, Traders and Craftworkers

John Hall, grocer

— Dunmore East, Co. Waterford

The world is not worth a fig,
I have good raisins for saying so.

An intelligent merchant

— A tombfellow of Richard McKenna above

Erected by the Merchants of Dundalk in memory of
JOHN CHAMBERS
who, during a residence among them of twenty years
maintained the character of a sincere friend, an
intelligent merchant, a valuable citizen and an Honest Man.
He died 7th August 1803.

O'Brien, the haberdasher

Here lies John O'Brien, sometime Hosier and Haberdasher.
He left his hose, his Anna and his love,
To sing Hosanna in the realms above.

The grand juryman

— *St Nicholas's Churchyard, Dundalk, Co. Louth*

Erected by public subscription to the memory of
RICHARD McKENNA
popular native of Dundalk, for many years in the service
of the Grand Jury of Louth, Died 3rd April 1899.
"Poor Richard, after life's fitful fever, he sleeps well."

The famed chairman

— *Dublin: Collected by Henry James Loaring, 1872.*

(The sedan-chair was introduced into Ireland in the eighteenth
century having first been used in the French city of Sedan. The
chair was carried on two poles by two chairmen, one in front and
one behind; it had a hinged door in front, windows at the sides and
a top which lifted so as to enable the occupant to stand up if he or
she chose, and to allow for the wearing of high head-dresses.)

Weep, Irish lads, all true and fair men;
Here rests the leader of the chairmen.

Reader, rejoice that here lies Pat,
For was he up he'd lay you flat.

In fame, you'll never see his brother,
It reach'd from one pole to the other.

And, would you know him when an angel fair,
You've nothing more to do than call, Chair! Chair!

The zealous locksmith

A zealous locksmith dy'd of late,
And did arrive at Heaven's gate,
He stood without and would not knock,
Because he meant to pick the lock.

Lines on a waggoner's tomb

Here lies the body of Nathaniel Parke,
Who never did no harm in the light, nor in the dark,
But in his blessed horses, taking great delight,
And often travelled with them by day and by night.

George Faulkner, printer

— Dublin, 1775

Turn, gentle stranger, and this urn revere,
O'er which Hibernia saddens with a tear.
Here sleeps GEORGE FAULKNER, printer once so dear
To humorous Swift, and Chesterfield's gay peer.

So dear to his wronged country and her laws;
So dauntless when imprisoned in her cause;
No alderman ere graced a weightier board,
No wit e're joked more freely with a lord
None could with him in anecdotes confer;
A perfect annal-book, in Elsevier.

Whate'er of glory life's first sheets presage,
Whate'er the splendour of the title page,
Leaf after leaf, though learned lore ensues;
Close as thy types and various as thy news;
Yet, George, we see that one lot awaits them all,
Gigantic folios, or octavos small
One universal finis claims his rank.
And every volume closes with a blank.

★ ★ ★

Epitaphs like this one which are a play on words were particularly popular in the eighteenth century. Here is one to be found all over Ireland:

The blacksmith's epitaph

My sledge and hammer lie declined,
My bellows-pipes have lost their wind,
My fire's extinct, my forge decay'd,
My vice is in the dust now laid;
My coal is spent, my iron's gone,
My nails are drove, my work is done,
My fire-dried corpse here lies at rest,
My soul, smoke-like, soars to be blest.

Legal all the way

— Mt Jerome, Dublin

An Col Tomás Mac Conmara
Croisín, Co An Cláir.
30-9-1916 go 23-9-1977.
A Gentleman by the Grace of God
and an Act of Parliament.

Dr Boyle Godfrey, died Dublin 1755: Doctor and Alchemist

Epitaphium Chymicum
Here lieth to digest, macerate, and amalgamate with clay,
In *Balneo Arenoe*
Stratum super Stratum,
The *Residium, Terra damnata* and *Caput Mortuum,*
of BOYLE GODFREY, Chymist and M.D.
A man, who, in this Earthly Laboratory, pursued various
Processes to obtain *Arcanum Vitae*
or the Secret to Live:
Also *Aurum Vitae*
Or, the art of getting rather than making gold.
Alchymist-like, all his Labour and Projection,
As Mercury in the Fire, Evaporated in Fume, when he
Dissolved to his first principles,
He departed as poor
As the last drops of an Alembic; for Riches are not
Poured on the Adepts of this world.
Though fond of News, he carefully avoided the
Fermentation, Effervescence, and Decrepitation of his life.
Full seventy years his Exalted Essence
Was hermetically sealed in its Terrene Matrass; but the
Radical Moisture being exhausted, the *Elixir Vitae* spent
And exciccated to a Cuticle, he could not suspend
Longer in his Vehicle, but precipitated Gradation, *per*
Camponan, to his original dust.
May that light, brighter than Bolognian Phospherous
Preserve him from the Athanor, Empyreuma, and Reverberatory
Furnace of the other world,
Depurate him from the Foecas and Scoria of this
Highly Rectify and Volatilize his aetherial spirit;
Bring it over the Helm of the Retort of this Globe, place
It in a proper Recipient or Crystalline orb,
Among the elect of the Flowers of Benjamine; never to
Be saturated till the Geneva Resuscitation.
Deflagration, Calcination and Sublimation of all things.

This delightful epitaph, a classic of its type, is redolent with the vocabulary of the alchemist, from Alembic (a distilling apparatus) to the *Elixir Vitae* (the liquid sought to prolong life).

A merchant from France

— *South Chapel, Cork*

Sargeant Malone, A Merchant from France,
Who valued the Riches of Life
As they secured him an interest in the next
And in 'The Lamb's Book of Life
Brought in Heaven a Debtor to Mercy,
And left the Ballance on the Table.'

The watchmaker
— *Limerick Cathedral*

Memento Mory
Here lieth little Samuel Barinton, that great Under
Taker,
Of Famous City's Clock and Chime Maker;
He made his one Time goe Early and Latter,
But now he is returned to God his Creator.
The 19 of November Thou he Seest,
And for his memory this here is pleast
By his Son Ben, 1693.

Watchmaking was a favourite theme on epitaphs:

Here lies in Horizontal position, the outside case
of George Routledge, Watchmaker,
Whose abilities in that line were an honour
to his profession:
Integrity was the Main-spring, and Prudence the
Regulator of all the Actions of his life:
Humane, generous, and liberal, his Hand never stopped
till he had relieved distress.
So sincerely Regulated were all his Movements, that
he never Went Wrong, except when Set a-going
by people who did not know his Key:
Even then he was easily Set Right again.
He had the art of
disposing this Time so well, that his hours
glided away in one continual Round of Pleasure and
Delight, till an unlucky Moment put a Period
to his existence.
He departed this life November 14th, 1802, aged 57.
Wound up in hopes of his being taken in hand by his
Maker, and of being thoroughly Cleaned, Repaired,
and Set a-going in the world to come.

Castle Caldwell, Lough Erne, Co. Cavan

To a drunken fiddler who drowned in the Lough — the memorial
tablet is in the shape of a violin:

AUGUST YE 15 1770
Beware ye fidlers of ye fidlers fate
Nor tempt ye deep least ye repeant to late
Ye ever have been deemed to water foes
Then shun ye lake till it with whiskey floes
On firm land only exercise your skill
There you may play and drink your fill.

The honest miller

— Kinnagh, Co. Wexford

Here lieth the body of
Anthony Reynolds a native of
The County Tyrone.
He was faithful to his employer
And, although a Miller was an honest man.
Departed this life December 13th, 1790, aged 33 years.

A Nod to the Wise

Two vacant spots

— *Belturbet, Co. Cavan*

Here lies JOHN HIGLEY
whose father and mother were drowned
in their passage from America.
Had they both lived they would have been buried here.

One of similar sentiment is to be found at Kilkeel, Co. Down:

Here lie the remains of Thomas Nichols
Who died in Philadelphia, March 1753.
Had he lived, he would have been buried here.

Who's he?

— *Ballina, Co. Mayo*

Here lies PAT STEELE
That's very true:
Who was he? What was he? —
What's that to you?
He lies here because he
Is dead — nothing new.

On Little Willie

— Dublin

Stranger weep, for at the age of seven,
Little Willie went to Heaven.

To which someone had added:

Cheer up, stranger, who can tell?
Willie may have gone to Hell.

The unfortunate Ulsterman

— Collected by Samuel Palmer, 1869

Erected to the memory of
JOHN PHILLIPS
Accidentally shot
As a mark of affection by his Brother.

Written by Patrick Leary, about his wife

— Belfast

Beneath this stone lies Katherine, my wife,
In death my comfort, and my plague through life.
Oh, liberty! But soft, I must not boast,
She'll haunt me else, by jingo, with her ghost.

Keep smiling

— Corofin, Co. Clare

In loving memory of Alice E Sharman, Born Valpariso, Chile
3rd Nov 1877. Died Corofin 25th Sept 1955.
Our heart is restless till it
Findeth rest in thee.
Audrey Douglas, Born Concepcion, Chile
January 25 1905. Died Cragmoher, July 20 1968.
Here as ever sleeping sound
Lies our Audrey in the ground
If she wakes as wake she may
There's be fun on Judgement Day.

Celestial take-away

— Adamstown, Co. Wexford

Erected by John Broder in memry of his nephew John Murphy
late of Camross who depd this live, Nov 6th 1835, agd 25 yrs.

God takes the good
Too good
On earth to stay
And leaves the bad
Too bad
To take away.

Celestial pop group

— All Saints Churchyard, Church of Ireland, Co. Wicklow

Sacred to the Memory of Henry Seymour
Son of Henry and Lucie Moore.
Who was born July 16th 1819
And called to his Heavenly home, May 8th 1823.
His mortal remains rest by the
Side of his sister whom he tenderly loved
And their angel spirits before the throne of God
Sing together their Redeemer's praise.

Still together

— Ballyhuskard, Co. Wexford

Erected by Laurence Redmond in memory of his
father
Patrick Redmond and Mother Margaret alias Sinnott
Depd this life Jan 19, 1819. He aged 79 & she 72
years.
Married we were upon a day and departed upon another.
Buried we were in native clay in both one day together.
Fifty years and two we lived in Marriage State
Reader pray for you Must sher death's certain Fate.

Had to go

— Clonattin, Co. Wexford

Erected by Mary Hughes Tuberduff in memory of her husband James Hughes, who dcpd April 4th 1856 aged 30 years.

> In love we lived, in peace we died
> I craved his life but God denied.

A favourite in Wexford

*— To be found at St Johns, Enniscorthy and Ramsgrange and
Fethard-on-Sea*

> How loved, how valued, it availeth thee not
> To whom related, or by whom begot.
> A heap of dust is all remains of thee
> Tis all thou art or all the proud shall be.

Make a choice

— Near Wellington Bridge, Kilcavan, Co. Wexford

Here lies the body of James Larken late of Kilcavan
who depd this life
May 1806 aged 21 years.

Pause Reader Pause upon these lines here given
On the torturing pains of Hell and joys of Heaven
One you have to chuse
Therefore take care what steps you are to take
And how you are to fare, therefore prepare for Heaven.
While here below ensure a long eternity of woe.

Darling Charlie

— Fethard-on-Sea, St Mogues, Co. Wexford

This dreary region contains Charles only beloved child
of Harriett Dixon. His gentle spirit left the arms of his
earthly advocate for the bosom of his Heavenly one on
6th of March, 1815, aged 15 years.

Dear Boy within this stone
The mother's hopes receive their doom.

Life is what you make it

— Glasnevin Cemetery, Dublin, on the tomb of the Delaneys

This is the best world that we live in,
To lend or to spend or to give in:
But to borrow or beg or to get a man's own,
It's the very worst world that ever was known.

Sudden calls

Under this stone lie two babies dear,
One is buried in Connaught, and t'other here.

★   ★   ★

Always tidy, always clean —
He lost his life in a submarine.

★   ★   ★

He was my husband, fond and dear;
Until he fell over Holy Cross weir.

★   ★   ★

Within this grave do lie
Back to back, my wife and I;
When the last trump the air shall fill,
If she gets up, I'll just lie still.

By the roadside

There's an old Irish story of the traveller who came across an old
man kneeling by the roadside praying to a milestone which read
'81 miles to Dublin'. When accosted the old man was told that he
was praying to a milestone, but he denied it to the traveller
vehemently, whereupon the traveller said, 'Well then read to me
what it says'. The old man read:

This man is dead and gone,
I hope his bones don't trouble him.
He died at the age of 81,
His name was Miles from Dublin.

The best will be

— Knockbrack Graveyard, Kesh, Co. Sligo

To the memory of John Kelly
who departed this life on the
12th Sept 1868 aged 55 years
after a life of labour but
with a mind at ease.

Remember man who'er thou art
Not he who acts the greatest part
But they who act the best will be
The happiest men eternally.

Smiles and tears are all the same

— Quin Abbey, Co. Clare

Reader, weep not, but pray
While time to thee is given
Your tears would only wet my clay
Your prayer may gain me heaven.

Someone thought about the sentiment and responded in rhyme ...

Friend, who speaks to us across the years,
You have our prayers, and not our tears;
We happened on your stone one sunlit day,
No doleful tears could thus damp down your clay;
Methinks your spirit mingled with our mirth,
For souls like thine must ever vanquish earth!
And when, in truth, we join you in a while
Methinks, dear friend, we'll know thee by thy smile.

Take care, me boys!

— John McAlaster of Plaster, Ballymascanlon, Co. Louth

His days dear Boys on earth were few —
They pass'd away like morning dew
Take learning by this calling youth
And early seek the God of truth.

An eye on the hourglass

— Corkbeg Churchyard, Co. Cork

To Michael Power
O Reader stay and cast an Eye
Upon this grave wherein I lie.
Cruel Death has conquered me,
And in a short time will conquer thee.
Repent in time make no delay,
For Christ will call us all away.
Time is scant; like dew in sun
Beyond all cure my glass is run.

Folks Known and Unknown

The Irish Giant

In Kilbroney graveyard, near Rostrevor, Co. Down, there stands a Celtic Cross to the memory of Patrick Murphy, who in his day was hailed as the tallest Irishman. His epitaph reads:

> Of your charity
> Pray for the Soul of
> Patrick Murphy of Kilbroney
> (The Irish Giant)
> To whose memory this monument
> has been erected
> By a few friends and admirers.

Patrick Murphy was born a countryman near the town of Rostrevor in June 1834. He attained the enormous height of 8ft 1in. Until the age of twenty, Murphy had been normal size, but then he suddenly sprouted. He earned his living in travelling circuses but succumbed to smallpox at Marseilles in April 1862. His body was embalmed and brought home for burial in a 9ft grave.

(More recent research, though, shows that the tallest Irishman on record was Patrick Cotter O'Brien [1760-1806] who was born at Kinsale, Co. Cork. His height was 8ft 7¾ins. This giant was only 'discovered' when his coffin was accidentally exposed during excavation work in Bristol; he had died at Hotwells, Clifton, Avon.)

Two wives, one grave

There is an epitaph to James Keally (1640) at Gowran, Co. Kilkenny, which recounts how he had been married twice and why he had just one vault built.

> Both wives at once alive he could not have,
> Both to enjoy at once he made this grave.

Lines on Richard Boardman

— Cork

Departed this life, October 4th, 1782.
***Aetatis* 44.**

Beneath this stone the dust of BOARDMAN lies,
His precious soul has soar'd above the skies;
With eloquence divine, he preach'd the word
To multitudes, and turn'd them to the Lord.

His bright example strengthened what he taught,
And devils trembled when for Christ he fought.
With truly Christian zeal he nations fired,
And all who knew him mourn'd when he expired.

On the Earl of Kildare

Who killed Kildare?
Who dare Kildare to kill?
Death killed Kildare,
Who dare kill whom he will.

John Gibson, Dean of Bangor

Co. Down has an interesting collection of epitaphs of the seventeenth century and Bangor Abbey has two of note. The first is still clearly legible in its original lettering:

HEIR LYES BELOVE (*below*) ANE LEARNED AND REVERAND FATHER IN GODES CHURCH MESTER JOHN GIBSON SENCE REFORMACION FROM POPARY THE FIREST DEANE OF DOWNE SEND BY HIS MAJESTIE INTO THIS KINGDOM AND RECEIVED BY MY LORD CLANEBOYE TO BE PREACHER AT BANGOR AT HIS ENTRY HAD XL COMMUNICANTES AND AT HIS DEPARTOUR THIS LYF 23 OF JUNII 1623 LEFT 1200 BEING OF AGE 63 YEARS SO CHRYST WAS HIS ADVANTAGE BOTHE IN LYFE AND DEATH.

The Bradshaw stone of 1620 records the burial of Thomas Bradshaw 'some tyme baillie in Bangour' and is a fine example of Jacobean work showing costume on the effigies. His epitaph reads:

Blessed are the dead
Which die in the Lord.
For they rest from
Their Labours and
Their Works.
Memento Mori.

Bradshaw's epitaph is a version of *Revelations* XIV.13 which reads: 'Blessed are the dead which die in the Lord from henceforth: Yea, saith the Spirit, that they may rest from their labours; and their works do follow them.' The Latin tag *Memento mori* (Remember that you must die) is usually, as in the Bradshaw case, accompanied by a human skull and crossbones, which have nothing to do with pirates!

Bangor Abbey also has a memorial to Beatrix Hamilton — the sister of Mrs Barbara Mean, wife of John Mean, an Edinburgh merchant; Mrs Mean was a herbwoman who threw her stool at the Dean of St Giles, Edinburgh, in 1637, for she objected to the *collect* he was to read, she being a loyal Presbyterian (popular tradition however gives this act to one 'Jenny Geddes').

The bodie of Beatrix heer below
In hope of Glorie doth now sweetly rest
Her soul hath soared wher floods of joy do flow
Of Sion that's above a glorious guest
Where Chrystal streams where Golden gleaming streets
Enjoy a constant day without a night
Where Jasper wher ports of peerless pearle
Embroidred are with the Lambs shining light
Thither I go, she said. This bodie fraile
Shal shortly in my coffin sweetly rest
Once sweet to thie, lot now to Christ. Farewell,
Wel meet I fully have whom I love best
O Blessed Covenant. Aweene for ay
Who was but a poore thing een yesterday.

Red Hugh, father of Macha who founded Emania

— Mullaghshee, Co. Donegal

TAIM-SE I'M CHODHLADHA
IS NA DUISIGH ME
(It's I am in my sleeping
And let you not wake me.)

Naughty Mary

— Co. Louth

Beneath these stones lie the Bones of Mary Jones,
But these are not the only stones that Mary Jones lay under.

Prince Eoghan, son of Niall

— Uisce-Chain, Inis Eoghain, Co. Donegal

Eoghan, son of Niall, died
Of tears — good his nature —
In consequence of the death of Conall, of hard feats.
So that his grave is at Uisce-Chain.

Dora's gone

— Foxhall cemetery, Carrigeen, Lenamore, Co. Longford

Sacred to the memory of Dora, wife of Emmet G Fox Esqr
Who died Christmas Day 1867, aged 26 years,
Death Shuck the Dart
And pitying sighed.
And virtue groaned
When Dora died.

Lines on a Servant

— St Patrick's Cathedral, Dublin

Here lieth the body of Alexander McGee, servant to
Doctor Swifte of St Patrick's. His grateful master
caused this monument to be erected in Memory of
Discretion, Fidelity and Diligence in that humble
Station. Ob. Mar 24 1723/24. Aetat. 29.

Some masters wanted it to be known how generous they had
been to their servants. On the tombstone of the Irish servant John
Quinny, who was in the service of Sir Henry Chester for fifty-six
years, were carved the words:

His master left him an annuity of £8.

The best medicine

— Cavangarden, Ballyshannon, Co. Donegal

Affliction sore, some time I bore,
Physicians tried in vain.
But God thought it best that I should rest
And eased me of my pain.

The British Minister

Robert Stewart Castlereagh, Viscount Castlereagh (1769-1822), born at Mountstewart, Co. Down, was a British Minister of War and Foreign Secretary. He took a leading part in the Napoleonic Wars, but was very unpopular. Lord Byron, the romantic poet, particularly disliked him, and wrote this on hearing that Castlereagh had died:

Posterity will ne'er survey
A nobler grave than this.
Here lie the bones of Castlereagh,
Stop, traveller — and p–s.

Just for a babe

— 1834: Anna Smith, Old Cathedral, Ardmore, Co. Waterford

Oh! sweet my baby liest thou here
So low, so cold and forsaken
And cannot a fond mother's tear
Thy once too lovely smile awaken.
Ah! now within this silent tomb
A mother's hopes received their doom
Ah! I shall ne'er forget the kiss
I gave thee on that morn of mourning
The placid cheek bespoke the bliss
Of innocence to God returning
May'st thou return that kiss to me
In realms of bright eternity.

Safe from Wave and Cannonball

Remembering the Warden

— St Nicholas's Churchyard, Dundalk, Co. Louth

Sacred to the memory of John Ingham late Quartr. Mafter 7th Dn Guards, who departed this life 22nd July, 1817, aged 62 years also of Elizabeth Ingham his wife who died 2nd Jany, 1818, aged 58 years this stone was erected as a tribute of filial love by their daughter Anne Ingham.

The Governors of the Louth Hospital have caused the following extract from their Journal to be engraved on the tombstone of their late Warden and Matron, John and Eliza Ingham. That we have just cause to lament their decease: That their conduct as Servants of the Public was uniformly regulated by the stricteft senfe of integrity and oeconomy and as Warden of the Sick and maimed by the tender feelings of tenderniss (*sic*): That in the care of the House generally they eftablished an admirable System of order alfo cleanliness and were both in their own behaviour Sober, Respectable and Decorous: That we are very desirous to uphold their example in all these respects for the imitation of those who may at any time hereafter succeed them.

From the same churchyard:

Sacred to the memory of David Williams who departed
this life the 18th day of March, 1824, aged 42 years.
This tribute of respect to a Departed Worth was placed
by his affectionate mother.

> Though boisterous winds and Neptune's waves
> Have tossed me to and from,
> In spite of both by God's decree
> I harbour here below.
>
> When now at anchor I do lie,
> With many of our fleet,
> In hope once more to set sail
> Our Saviour Christ to meet.

The epitaph to David Williams mirrors the sentiment of other
epitaphs to be found in the coastal graveyards of Ireland, or
wherever sailors are buried. Here are some more:

> At anchor now in Death's dark road,
> Rides honest Captain Hill,
> Who served his King and feared his God,
> With upright heart and will.

In social life sincere and just,
To vice of no kind given;
So that his better part, we trust,
Hath made the Port of Heaven.

★   ★   ★

Tho' Boreas with his blust'ring blasts,
Has tost me to and fro,
Yet by the handywork of God,
I'm here inclos'd below.

And in this silent bay I lie
With many of our fleet,
Untill the day that I set sail,
My Admiral Christ to meet.

★   ★   ★

At Kililagh, Co. Clare, some of the crewmen of the Spanish Armada are buried. Their epitaph simply states:

TAUMPLE NA SPANIG
(Burial place of the Spaniards)

★   ★   ★

And who would fail to understand this:

Here I lies,
Killed by the X.I.S. (the Excise!)

***In memory of Trumpet Major Keeling, 8th Hussars, killed by a
fall from his horse***

— Newbridge Churchyard, Co. Galway

Of Nature's chain one link lies buried here,
A soldier truthful, honest and sincere,
By many known, by all beloved was he,
His maxims true, his maxim honesty.

In prime of life death stopped his bright career,
Today in health, tomorrow on his bier.
Then rest ye, KEELING, rest, nor fear the route,
Till the last trumpet sounds the great 'Turn-out'.

For his posterity

— Monknewton, Drogheda, Co. Louth

Erected to Patrick Kelly
Of the Town of Drogheda, Mariner.
In Memory of his Posterity.

Also the above Patrick Kelly
who departed this Life the 12th August 1844.
Aged 60 years.
Requiescat in Pace

Just for peace

— Brass, in the Church of the Immaculate Conception, Camolin, Co. Wexford

As the days roll by, this day we do recall.
The noonday sun.
The twittering of strange birds.
The brown meandering stream, that heard the din of battle
And carried your cries to history, to join the brave.
That swords be turned into ploughshares.

Erected by the people of Camolin and comrades
To the memory of Trooper Edward Gaffney, Norrismount.
Killed in the Congo (Zaire) on the 13th September 1961.
In the cause of world peace.

John Hall of Dunleary, Sailor

Through Boreas' spight and Neptune's foom,
I have ranged ye Ocean wide, by God's decree
it is my doom.
October 3rd, 1750.

A watery demise

— Marmullane Graveyard, Co. Cork

Timothy Connell, mariner, murdered 1828 on the
Mary Russell out of Cork, by the ship's master.

You gentle reader that do pass this way
Attend a while, adhere to what I say.
By murder vile I was bereft of life
And parted from two lovely babes and wife.
By Captain Stewart I met an early doom
On board the Mary Russell the 22nd of June.
Forced from the world to meet my God on High
With whom I hope to reign eternally.

Nelson's compatriot

— *St Patrick's, Creeach, Glendum Rd, Cushendun, Co. Antrim*

On John McAlaster who served with Lord Nelson against the French:

HERE LIES THE BOODY OF JOHN ... DIED 11 MARCH 1803
AGED 18 YEARS
YOUR SHIP, LOVE, IS MORED, HEAD AND STARN, FOR A
FUL DIEW.

A lush in dock

— *Knockbrack Graveyard, Keash, Co. Sligo*

John Cullen, mariner, died in 1878 aged 62, all his life he fought the sea and the bottle:

**For 35 years and upwards
I fought king alcohol.
With heart in hand
And tongue in a foreign land.
And I won the victory.
I am back again in the old country
Fighting the same old king
And so far I am victorious.**

Exiles All

Across the pond

A gregarious folk, the Irish have turned up all over the world in search of fame and fortune, and their epitaphs in desert and shady churchyard plot their wanderings and last resting places be they in Melbourne, Australia, or Monterey, Mexico. Thousands of Irish men and women were fired by the nineteenth-century gold rushes in America and their epitaphs make up a large ethnic group in the appropriately named Death Valley in California. Here are some recorded in an old goldminer's logbook:

MARTHA MAYS OF THE GOLD NUGGET SALOON
Here lies the body of Martha Mays
Who was so virginal in stays,
She lived to the age of three score and ten
And gave to the worms what she refused to the men.

WHISKEY JOE
He had some faults
And many merits
He died of drinking
Home brewed spirits.

ANDY MONNEY'S WIFE
Here lies my poor wife,
A bitch and a shrew
If I said I missed her
I should lie too.

HANNAH'S THREE IN A ROW
This Old rock has drunk a widow's tear
Three of my husbands are buried here.

PETE CONNOR WROTE THIS ON HIS WIFE
**Who far below in this grave doth rest
She's join'd the army of the blest;
The Lord has ta'en her to the sky,
The saints rejoice, and so do I.**

FAT MAY PRESTON
Here lies the body of
Fat May Preston
Who's now moved to heaven
To relieve the congestion.

UNLUCKY BILL SMEE
**Here lies Will Bill Smee
Who ran for sheriff in '83
He also ran in '84
But ain't a runnin' any more.**

CHARLOTTE O'RILEY OF COPPERSTONE CREEK
Here lie the bones of Copperstone Charlotte
Born a virgin, died a harlot.
For sixteen years she kep' her virginity
A darn'd long time in this vicinity.

RHYMIN' PETE
Living and dying I loved the truth
And I'll speak it now, though it seem uncouth;
I wrote thirty poems, and was published as well,
So I don't care now if it's Heaven or Hell.

LARRY THE LUSH
Here lie the earthly remains of
Larry G Chappell.
He hath joined the spirits
Of which he was always so fond.

PERCY THE PRETTY BOY
The mortal remains of Percy Claud Crintle
Lie in the dust under this old lintle.
He worked with us all without any shame
And all he had left was his pretty name.

There must be a certain opportunistic streak in the Irish soul, for the graveyards of America show how even in death the Irish were not against advertising:

Oxford, New Hampshire

Here lies Jane Smith, widow of Thomas Smith, marblecutter; this monument was erected by her husband as a tribute to her memory and a specimen of his work. Monuments of the same style 250 dollars.

★　★　★

Died on the 11th inst, at his shop, No 20 Greenwich St, Mr Edward Jones, much respected by all who knew and dealt with him. As a man he was amiable; as a hatter upright and moderate. His virtues were beyond all price, and his beaver hats were only three dollars each. He has left a widow to deplore his loss, and a large stock to be sold cheap, for the benefit of his family. He was snatched to the other world in the prime of life, just as he had concluded an extensive purchase of felt; which he got so cheap that his widow can supply hats at more reasonable rates than any house in the city. His disconsolate family will carry on business with punctuality.

And in the same graveyard, an Irish packman:

> To all my friends I bid adieu;
> A more sudden death you never knew;
> As I was leading the old mare to drink,
> She kick's and kill'd me quicker'n a wink.

Brawne, the Irish beggar, who tramped the Cornish byways:

> Here Brawne, the quondam beggar lies,
> Who counted by his tale,
> Some six score winters and above:
> Such virtue is in ale.
>
> Ale was his meate, his drinke, his cloth,
> Ale did his death reprieve;
> And could he still have drunk his ale,
> He has been still alive.

O'Neills in Rome

In exile Prince Rory O'Donnell, Earl of Tyrconnell (d. 29 July 1608), and his brother Caffar (d. 15 Oct. 1608), and Hugh, Baron of Dungannon (d. 1 Oct. 1608), nephew of the Earl of Tyrconnell all lie in the Church of St Peter, Montorio, Italy. Their epitaphs were in Latin. Hugh's read:

HIC QUIESCUNT HUGONIS PRINCIPIS O'NEILL OSSA.

Canadian speedster (on the grave of a young Irishman who had a weakness for motorbikes):

> **He sped himself to an early grave**
> **Never to enjoy the time he saved.**

The Irish peeress at Pewsey, Bedforshire

> Here lies the body of
> Lady O'LOONEY,
> Great-niece of Burke, commonly
> called the Sublime.
> She was
> Bland, passionate, and deeply religious;
> Also she painted in water colours,
> And sent several pictures to the Exhibition.
> She was the first cousin to Lady Jones,
> And such is the kingdom of heaven.

On an Irishman who drove an armoured train at Kimberley

> No more will he stand on the footplate,
> No more will he steam into town.
> He has shut off his steam for ever,
> And gone to pick up his crown.

The Valiant Captain Tully: Exeter Cathedral

Here lies the body of Captain Tully,
Aged an hundred and nine years fully;
And threescore years before, as Mayor,
The sword of this city he did bear;
Nine of his wives do with him lie,
So shall the tenth when she doth die.

The tomb of an Irish mercenary at Lille

Oh, Cruel Death, to make three meals in one,
To taste and taste till all was gone.
But know, thou Tyrant, when the trump shall call
He'll find his feet and stand when thou shall fall.

(Apparently this soldier first lost a toe through gangrene, afterwards a leg, and then his life.)

From Kohat, Afghanistan

Here rests the remains of Michael Healy, Apothecary in the Hon'ble Company's service, destroyed by the Afreedees 22nd March 1850. Michael Healy was an Irishman, highly gifted with talents, energy and ambition. Foiled in his aim and weary of his struggle with the world, he ardently sought that repose which he has here found.

(The Afreedees were an Afghan tribe, and the 'Hon'ble Company' mentioned was the Honourable East India Company which had been founded by royal charter in 1600; many Irishmen were to be found in its service).

Irish Writers and the Epitaph

Many of Ireland's celebrated writers have tried out the epitaph form as a part of their writing either as poetry, or satire, or as memorials to their friends. For instance the playwright Michael Clancey wrote this of Thomas Tickell, aged 54, 1740:

> Read Tickell's name, and gently tread the clay
> Where lie his sole Remains that could decay!
> Then pensive sigh, and through fair Science trace,
> His mind adorn'd with every pleasing Grace.
> Worth such as Rome would have confessed her own;
> Wit, such as Athens would have proudly shown.
> Substance to thought, and weight to fancy joined;
> A judgement perfect, and a Taste refined
> Admired by God, by Addison beloved
> Esteemed by Swift, by Pope himself approv'd;
> His spirit, rais'd by that Sublime he knew,
> Hence to the seat of bright Perfection flew,
> Leaving, to sorrowful Clotilda here,
> A mournful Heart, and never-ceasing tear.

Some like William Butler Yeats wrote epitaphs for themselves. His is to be found on his gravestone in Drumcliff Churchyard, near Sligo, and reads:

> **Cast a cold eye**
> **On life, on death.**
> **Horseman, pass by.**

It was the friends of George Moore the novelist who set up these lines for him at Castle Island, Lough Carra:

> Born Moore Hall, 1852. Died 1933, London.
> He forsook his family and friends for his art
> but because he was faithful to his art
> his family and friends
> reclaimed his ashes for Ireland.
> *Vale*

The 'autograph tree' at Coole, signed by W. B. Yeats,
G. B. Shaw and other writers.

Mrs Felicia Dorothea Hemans, the poet, buried at Dublin, was given a more traditional 'literary' epitaph:

> Calm on the bosom of thy God,
>   Fair spirit, rest thee now:
> Even while with us thy footstep trod,
>   His seal was on thy brow.
>
> Dust! to its narrow house beneath!
>   Soul! to its place on high!
> They that have seen thy look in death
>   No more may fear to die.

Writing in the celebrated *Notes & Queries* in 1929, one correspondent ascribed by family repute these two epitaphs to Jonathan Swift:

> **Here lies the body of John Shine,**
> **Who was no Jew for he ate swine;**
> **He was no Papist for he had no merit;**
> **He was no Quaker for he had no spirit;**
> **For forty years he lived and lied,**
> **For which God damned him as he died.**

*   *   *

> Here lie the bones of honest Peg,
> Who had no issue but in her leg;
> She was wondrous wise and cunning,
> For when one leg stopt t'other kept running.

Again this epitaph is attributed to Swift on an unknown lady:

> Here lies a lady, who if not bely'd,
> St Paul's advice took up, and all things try'd;
> Nor stopp'd she here, but follow'd through the rest,
> And always stuck the longest to the best.

Swift's ready wit was said by Victorian epitaph scholars to have been the foundation of these lines in Berkeley Churchyard, Gloucestershire, on Richard Pearce:

> Here lies the Earl of Suffolk's Fool,
> Men call'd him Dicky Pearce;
> His Folly serv'd to make Folks laugh,
> When Wit and Mirth were scarce.
>
> Poor Dick, alas! is dead and gone,
> What signifies to cry?
> Dicky's enough are still behind,
> To laugh at by and by.

Buried June 18, 1728, aged 63

He was less jocular about Judge Godfrey Boate (1673-1721) the Irish lawyer:

> **Here lies JUDGE BOATE within a coffin:**
> **Pray, gentle folks, forbear your scoffing.**
> **A *boat*, a *judge!* Yes, where's the blunder?**
> **A *wooden* judge is no such wonder!**
> **And in his robes you must agree,**
> **No boat was better deckt than he.**
> **T'is needless to describe him fuller;**
> **In short, he was an able *sculler*.**

Dean Swift showed his scorn for both Gilbert Burnet, Bishop of Salisbury, who died in 1715, and for the Duke and Duchess of Marlborough in his famous 'Here Sarum lies':

Here Sarum lyes
Who was as wise
And learned as Tom Aquinas.
Lawn sleeves he wore
Yet was no more
A Christian than Socinus.

Oaths pro and con
He Swallow's down
Loved Gold like any lay man
Wrote Preached and pray'd
And yet betrayed
God's Holy Church for Mammon.

Of every Vice
He had a Spice
Altho' a learned Prelate
And yet he dyed
If not belyed
A true Dissenting Zealote.

If such a Soule
To Heaven he's stole
And scaped old Satan's Clutches
We then assume
There may be room
From M[arborough] and his D[uches]s.

Swift on Partridge, the Almanac Maker, died 1708:

> Here, five feet deep, lies on his back
> A cobbler, starmonger and quack;
> Who, to the stars in pure good will;
> Does to his best look upward still.
> Weep, all you customers that use
> His pills, his almanacs, or shoes;
> And you that did your fortune seek,
> Step to his grave but once a week;
> This earth, which bears his body's print
> You'll find has so much virtue in't,
> That I durst pawn my ears 'twill tell
> Whate'er concerns you full as well,
> In physick, stolen goods, or love,
> As he himself could, when above.

The Dean also wrote an epitaph to show up the meanness of some relatives:

Underneath lies the body of Frederick, Duke of Schomberg, slain at the Battle of the Boyne, in the year 1690. The Dean and Chapter of this Church again and again besought the Heirs of the Duke to cause some monument to be here erected to his memory. But when, after many entreaties by letters and by friends they found they could not obtain this Request, they themselves placed this stone; only that the indignant Reader may know where the ashes of Schomberg are deposited. Thus did the Fame only of his Virtue obtain more for him from strangers, that nearness of blood from his own Family.

Swift on John D'Amory, the Usurer, died 1720.

Beneath this verdant Hillock lies
Demar the wealthy and the wise.
His heirs, that he might safely rest,
Have put his carcase in a chest
The very chest, in which, they say
His other self, his money, lay.
And if his heirs continue kind
To that dear self he left behind.
I dare believe that four in five
Will think his better self alive.

Jonathan Swift wrote this epitaph for himself and it is still to be seen in the vestiaries, St Patrick's Cathedral, Dublin:

Hic depositum est Corpus
JONATHAN SWIFT S.T.D.
Hujus Ecclesia Cathedralis
Decani
Ubi saeva Indignatio
Ulterius
Cor lacerare nequit
Abi Viator
Et imicare, si poteris
Strenuum pro virili
Libertatis vindicatorem
Obiit 19 Die Mensis Octobris
AD 1745. Anno Aetatis 78.

(The latter lines, or course, being added on his death.)

Underneath lie
interred the mortal remains
of Mrs HESTER JOHNSON better
known to the world by the Name of STELLA
under which she is celebrated in the writings of
Dr JONATHAN SWIFT dean of this cathedral
She was a Person of Extraordinary Endow-
ments and Accomplishments in body, mind & behaviour; justly admired and respected, by all who
knew her, on account of her many eminent virtues, as well as for her great natural and
acquired Perfections.
She dyed January the 27th 1727—8
in the 46th year of her Age and
by her will bequeathed one
thousand Pounds towards the
Support of a Chaplain to
the Hospital founded in
this City by Doctor
Steevens.

The epitaph may be translated thus:

Here is deposited the corpse of
JONATHAN SWIFT, Doctor of Sacred Theology,
of this cathedral church,
Dean.
Where the heart is unable any further
to be lacerated by savage indignation.
[*And you, a*] traveller [*to some unspecified
destination, are to*] go [*away,*] and [*to*] imitate,
if you are able, a strenuous vindicator of liberty,
[*to the utmost of something not stated, but presumably of your
ability.*]

He died on the 19th day of the month of October in the year of our
Lord 1745, in the year of his age 78.

This epitaph acted as an inspiration to W. B. Yeats who gave his own 'free' translation:

> Swift sailed into his rest;
> Savage indignation there
> Cannot lacerate his breast.
> Imitate him, if you dare,
> World-besotted traveller; he
> Served human liberty.

The Rev. Patrick Brontë (formerly Brunty), born in 1777 at Emdale, Loughbrickland, Co. Down, is not remembered today as a poet, as are his more famous children Charlotte, Emily, Anne and Patrick. But he allowed the Irish muse to inspire him to write an epitaph on his friend the Rev. Miles Oddy who died in 1841:

> Firm in the Faith, he heavenward held his way,
> Unchecked by fell relapse, or dull delay.
> In trials keen, he shrank not from the rod,
> He owned the Father in the chastening God;
> And when a ray of joy divinely shone,
> He gave the praise to God, and God alone.
> In friendship firm and true, to none a foe,
> He had that calm, which bad men never know.
> The Cross of Christ, was aye, his glowing theme,
> Illumin'd by the spirit's heavenly beam;
> And as he preach'd he liv'd and show'd the road,
> That leads to peace on earth, and joy with God.
> Then, reader, think, believe, repent and pray;
> That, so, through Grace Divine, on the Last Day,
> You may, triumphal, wear a Crown of Gold,
> When Christ shall all the Deity unfold;
> Whilst countless saints and angels heavenly raise
> Their heavenly notes of wonder, love and praise.

Although Oliver Goldsmith was buried at the Temple Church, London, and commemorated in Westminster Abbey, no anthology of Irish epitaphs would be complete without including him. This is his epitaph written by Samuel Johnson. The actual memorial was destroyed in the air raid on the church in May 1941:

SODALIUM AMOR	By the love of his associates
AMICARUM FIDES	The fidelity of his friends
LECTORUM VENERATIO	And the veneration of his readers
HOC MONUMENTUM	This monument is raised to the
MEMORIAM COLUIT	memory of
OLIVARII GOLDSMITH	OLIVER GOLDSMITH
POETAE, PHYSICI,	A poet, a natural philosopher,
HISTORICI	a historian
QUI NULLUM FERE	Who left no species of writing
SCRIBENDI GENUS NON	untouched by his pen.
TETIGIT	
NULLUM QUOT TETIGIT	Nor touched any that he did not
NON ORNAVIT	embellish.
SIVE RESUS ESSENT	Whether smiles or tears were to
MOVENDI	be excited,
SIVE LACRYMAE	He was a powerful yet gentle
AFFECTUUM POTENS, AT	master over the affections;
LENIS DOMINATOR	Of a genius at once sublime,
INGENIO SUBLIMIS,	lively, equal to every subject.
VIVIDUS VERSATILES	In expression at once lofty,
	elegant, and graceful.
NATUS IN HIBERNIA	He was born in Ireland
IN LOCO QUI NOMEN PALLAS	At a place called Pallas
FORNEIAE	In the parish of Forney,
LONGFORDIENSIS	county Longford
NOV XXIX MDCCXXXI	29th November 1731
EBLANAE LITERIS	Educated at Dublin
INSTITUTUS	
OBIIT LONDINI	Died in London
APRIL IV MDCCLXXIV	April 4 1744

Three months after Goldsmith's death, Samuel Johnson wrote this epitaph in memory of him in Greek:

> Whoe'er thou art, with reverence tread
> Where Goldsmith's letter'd dust is laid
> If nature and the historic page,
> If the sweet muse thy care engage
> Lament him dead, whose powerful mind
> Their various energies combin'd.

Goldsmith, too, wrote epitaphs on others.

JOHN NEWBURY, PUBLISHER, D. 1767

> What we say of a thing that has just come in fashion,
> And that which we do with the dead,
> Is the name of the honestest man in the nation:
> What more of a man can be said?

Here's what Goldsmith composed for the tomb of the portrait painter Sir Joshua Reynolds (1723-92):

> **Here Reynolds is laid, and, to tell you my mind,**
> **He has not left a wiser or better behind;**
> **His pencil was striking, resistless and grand;**
> **His manners were gentle, complying and bland.**
> **Still born to improve us in every part,**
> **His pencil our faces — his manners our heart;**
> **To coxcombs averse, yet most civilly steering;**
> **When they judge without skill, he was still hard of**
> **hearing;**
> **When they talked of their Raphaels, Correggios and stuff,**
> **He shifted his trumpet and only took snuff.**